LaFosse & Alexander's

DOLLAR ORIGAMI

Michael G. LaFosse and Richard L. Alexander

TUTTLE Publishing

Tokyo | Rutland, Vermont | Singapore

The Tuttle Story
"Books to Span the East and West"

Most people are surprised to learn that the world's largest publisher of books on Asia had its humble beginnings in the tiny American state of Vermont. The company's founder, Charles E. Tuttle, belonged to a New England family steeped in publishing. And his first love was naturally books—especially old and rare editions.

Immediately after WW II, serving in Tokyo under General Douglas MacArthur, Tuttle was tasked with reviving the Japanese publishing industry. He later founded the Charles E. Tuttle Publishing Company, which thrives today as one of the world's leading independent publishers.

Though a westerner, Tuttle was hugely instrumental in bringing a knowledge of Japan and Asia to a world hungry for information about the East. By the time of his death in 1993, Tuttle had published over 6,000 books on Asian culture, history and art—a legacy honored by the Japanese emperor with the "Order of the Sacred Treasure," the highest tribute Japan can bestow upon a non-Japanese.

With a backlist of 1,500 titles, Tuttle Publishing is more active today than at any time in its past—inspired by Charles Tuttle's core mission to publish fine books to span the East and West and provide a greater understanding of each.

Published by Tuttle Publishing, an imprint of Periplus Editions (HK) Ltd.

www.tuttlepublishing.com

Copyright © 2013 by Michael G. LaFosse and Richard L. Alexander
These origami models may not be used for commercial purposes without written permission from the authors.

ISBN 978-0-8048-4274-7

Library of Congress cataloging in process.

DISTRIBUTED BY
North America, Latin America & Europe
Tuttle Publishing
364 Innovation Drive, North Clarendon, VT 05759-9436 U.S.A.
Tel: (802) 773-8930 | Fax: (802) 773-6993
info@tuttlepublishing.com | www.tuttlepublishing.com

Japan
Tuttle Publishing
Yaekari Building, 3rd Floor, 5-4-12 Osaki, Shinagawa-ku, Tokyo 141 0032
Tel: (81) 3 5437-0171 | Fax: (81) 3 5437-0755
sales@tuttle.co.jp | www.tuttle.co.jp

Asia Pacific
Berkeley Books Pte. Ltd.
61 Tai Seng Avenue #02-12, Singapore 534167
Tel: (65) 6280-1330 | Fax: (65) 6280-6290
inquiries@periplus.com.sg | www.periplus.com

First edition
17 16 15 14 13   6 5 4 3 2 1   130510
Printed in China

TUTTLE PUBLISHING® is a registered trademark of Tuttle Publishing, a division of Periplus Editions (HK) Ltd.

Contents

Introduction

Dollar bill origami, or cleverly folded cash, continues to grow in popularity as people realize how much fun it is. Our printed U.S. currency is easy to fold, remarkably durable, intricately decorated, and globally ubiquitous. It is the most handy of all origami materials, and quickly becomes a fun pastime or social ice-breaker, especially when you may be killing a few minutes while waiting for someone or something.

We all relate to the "greenback." Our first childhood allowance for becoming responsible for routine household or pet chores probably gave us the bills we held for the longest time. Children must save several weeks' worth of cash to purchase something valuable, and in the interim, the precious bills are scrutinized, counted, and now, often folded. We often assure our young folders, who worry about "using up" their cash by folding it, that they can quickly unfold it and spend it. In fact, if they have ever spent dollar bills without folding them first, they have not gotten their full enjoyment from their money!

Perhaps this is why young visitors to our Origamido Studio; to the wildly popular *Origami Now!* exhibition at the Peabody Essex Museum in Salem, Massachusetts; to our Origami Do Experience—Waikiki; or to the Coolidge Crafts Exhibition Hall at Topsfield Fair were particularly captivated by the display of dozens of origami objects cleverly folded from cash.

There are now a respectable number of talented origami designers and authors who specialize in time-consuming, super-complex, magnificent manipulations of money, but we strongly feel that folding a bill to become a simple and attractive tip need not take three hands and a day off.

We recognized how wonderful the simple dollar bill folds were for introducing people to the fascinating world of folding, and our *Money Origami* DVD kit was Tuttle Publishing's first foray into including our video instructions along with the printed diagrams in an origami kit. It quickly became their best selling title! We followed up with a *Mini Money Origami* DVD kit, and added a couple of projects with a touch more challenge to build on the basic skills represented by the simple selections in our popular primer kit.

This *Dollar Origami* book and DVD builds upon the lessons and skills presented in our first two money origami kits. We have included a few new, simple and fresh folds for those who may have missed out on exploring our first kit (or for when you need to produce something quickly), but we have also tried to raise the bar to create charming new models that intermediate folders will cherish as cash classics. We have also revisited the oft overlooked, yet extremely popular family of designs—multi-piece constructions assembled from multiple bills all folded the same way.

We always enjoy compiling our favorite dollar-based creations, and regularly come up with new models that we can't wait to share. We hope you have fun folding our new offerings: Our rocket and rabbits, the "Reef Pony" sea horse, and Michael's cuddly teddy bear are sure to delight your family and friends. Whether you are making a collection for your own display, decorating a holiday tree, giving cash in a unique way, or simply saying thanks for a small favor, we hope these new designs will soon become part of your origami repertoire.

Enjoy each piece of your money multiple times, and then use them to put a smile on the next face to see them!

—Origamido, Inc.
Richard L. Alexander and Michael G. LaFosse

Origami Symbols Key

Our diagrams use the standard origami notations that are shown here. If you are new to origami notation, please be encouraged that the project diagrams are complete and clear. However, your ability to easily interpret them will take time, like learning to read any foreign language. Studying from both the video lessons and the diagrams will help you to learn to read origami instructions much more quickly.

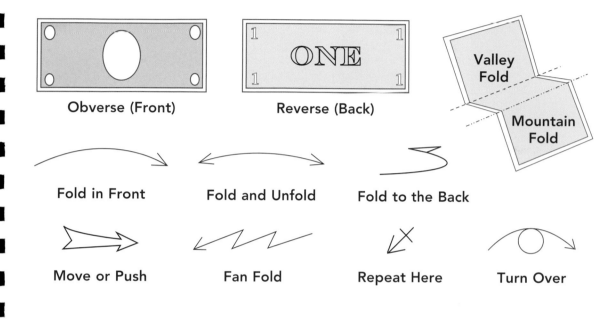

Obverse (Front) Reverse (Back) Valley Fold Mountain Fold

Fold in Front Fold and Unfold Fold to the Back

Move or Push Fan Fold Repeat Here Turn Over

General Tips

Clean, crisp money is easier to fold, and new bills always work best. When selecting a bill for an origami subject, look for one that is printed symmetrically (equal margins all around, and the printed images are registered so that the fields align when held to the light). If your bills are limp, they can be gently ironed, but first place them between sheets of paper so the plastic inclusions do not mar the iron's hot surface.

U.S. one dollar bills are remarkably strong, and for origami, they tend to be a bit stiff. For this reason, most dollar bill folders add a slight amount of moisture, either by swiping the bill with a moist napkin or towel, or with just a light spritz from a plant mister.

Consider gathering a few tools to make your results look neat and crisp: 1) a "bone" folder helps when setting sharp creases—or a coin, or even the bowl of a spoon; 2) a pair of fine tweezers helps to pull edges into proper alignment, and details into final position; 3) a bamboo skewer is useful for opening eyes and mouths on your miniature creatures; and 4) a pair of nylon jaw jewelers' pliers will help you concentrate force to properly set multi-layer points and flaps.

Lee's Coin Pouch

Designed by Richard L. Alexander

My father, Lee Alexander, has carried a rubbery plastic clamshell coin pouch ever since they were first developed. They used to be a popular tangible advertising item, and by carrying just a few coins, it prevented him from receiving handfuls of coins as change. Folding a similar object from a dollar bill goes one step further: It is lighter, thinner, and more compact. But best of all, if you get in a pinch, you will always have one dollar more than the sum of its contents!

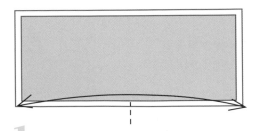

1 Begin with the obverse side up. Mark the center of a long edge with a short valley fold pinch mark.

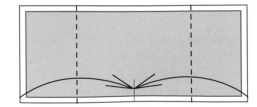

2 Valley-fold the short edges to meet at the middle.

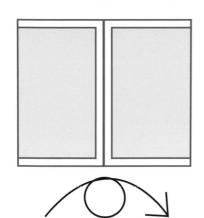

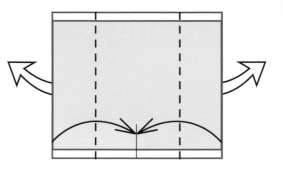

4 Valley-fold the folded edges to meet at the middle. Allow the back edges to come to the front.

3 Turn over, left to right.

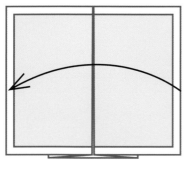

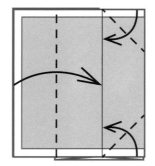

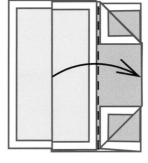

5 Move the top right flap to the left.

6 Valley-fold the corners of the right flap to the vertical crease. Valley-fold the left edge of the top flap the vertical crease.

7 Valley-fold the left flap to the right.

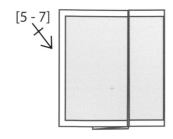

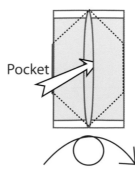

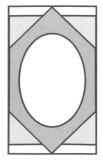

[5 - 7]

Pocket

8 Mirror steps 5 through 7 on the left.

9 Open the pocket through the folded slit. This is the back of the coin pouch. Turn over.

10 Lee's Coin Pouch.

Canoe

Designed by Richard L. Alexander

There must be a million ways to float the dollar, but this is one that our government probably hasn't tried yet. This may be the simplest of many one dollar canoes, and we hope it will become the springboard for a flotilla of more complex cash craft from you, Creative Captains of Crease. It makes a great chopsticks rest.

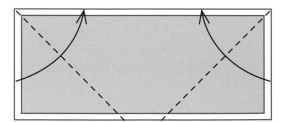

1 Begin with the obverse side up for a green canoe. Valley-fold the left and right short edges to the top edge.

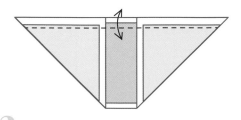

2 Valley-fold all of the layers of the top edge down to form a folded margin. Unfold.

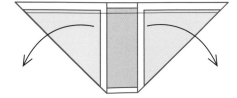

3 Unfold the left and right triangle flaps.

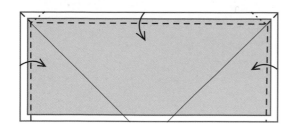 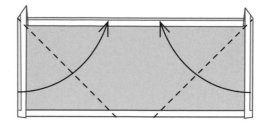

4 Use the perimeter creases to valley-fold the top and side edges in, while folding the top corners in half and flattening them to lay above the top edge. Look at the next diagram for the shape.

5 Use the diagonal creases to valley-fold the left and right triangle flaps up.

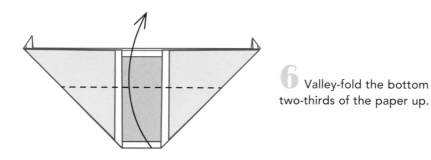

6 Valley-fold the bottom two-thirds of the paper up.

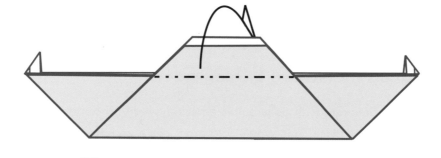

7 Mountain-fold the top flap down into the canoe.

8 The Canoe.

Windmill Pillow Tile

Designed by Richard L. Alexander

We love to decorate with dollars. It is amazing what you can do by folding crisp bills just once or twice. This simple fold produces a variety of interesting tilings, and can even be used to form larger squares to be use for wrapping small gifts, or to fold thousands of conventional origami subjects.

You will need four U.S. bills, of any denomination or combination, thereof.

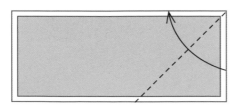

1 Begin obverse side up. Valley-fold the short right edge up to the top long edge.

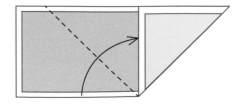

2 Valley-fold the bottom edge to meet with the vertical edge of the triangle flap.

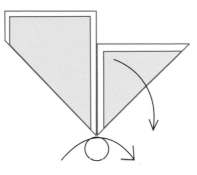

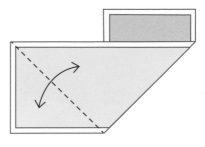

3 Your paper should look like this. Unfold the triangle flap and turn the paper over, left to right.

4 Valley-fold the existing mountain crease to exercise it.

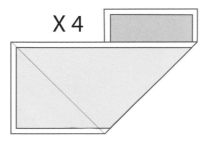

X 4

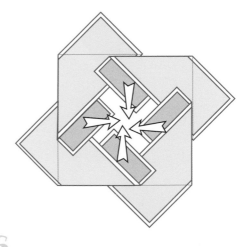

5 You will need four folded elements, like this one.

6 Arrange and overlap the units so that each is at a cardinal point of the compass: north, south, east and west. Slide together to close the center. Look at the next diagram to confirm the arrangement.

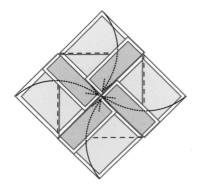

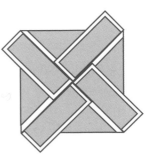

7 Valley-fold each of the four triangle flaps, tucking them under the center, rectangular flaps.

8 The Windmill Pillow Tile.

Lantern Puzzle

Designed by Richard L. Alexander

Do not try this at home (without using crisp, strong bills)! Our local banks carry fresh cash in December, since giving money never goes out of style. Here is a perfect pedestal for another origami creation, and it can also be used as a frame or cage to set off another dollar bill masterpiece. They stack to make a statement, and the simple fold teaches the beginner manual dexterity, as well as how important it is to set the creases crisply and the angles precisely. Sloppy folding makes this puzzle nearly impossible to complete.

You will need three bills. When folded from higher denomination bills, it will really light up a face!

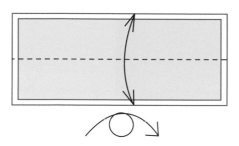

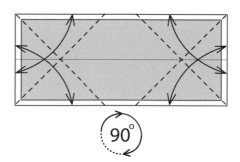

1 Begin with the reverse side up. Valley-fold in half, long edge to long edge. Unfold. Turn over, left to right.

2 Valley-fold each end of the bill in 45 degree diagonals by folding the short ends to the top and the bottom long edges, unfolding after each. Rotate the paper 90 degrees.

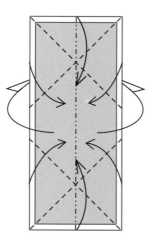

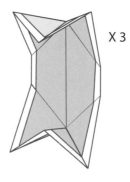

X 3

3 Use the crease pattern to mountain- and valley-fold the paper in the form shown in step 4.

4 You will need three units folded like this one.

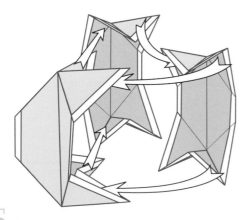

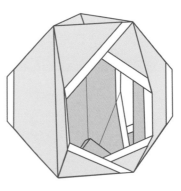

5 Weave the three units together by inserting the top and bottom left-side corners of one puzzle piece into the top and bottom right-side corners of another.

6 The Lantern Puzzle.

George Washington Monument

Designed by Richard L. Alexander

When this simple model is folded and assembled from four bills, you have a respectable dollar bill replica of the famous obelisk in Washington, D.C. Add four more bills below, and you are on your way to leaving a monumental tip—especially if you fold it from fives or tens!

You will need four bills to make a one-level "classic" monument (shown on the left).

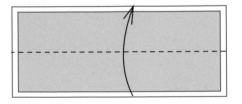

1 Begin with the preferred display side down. Valley-fold in half, long edge to long edge.

2 Mark the middle of one end of the folded bill with a short valley crease.

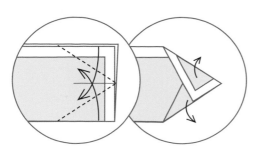

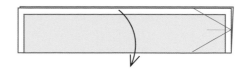

3 Valley-fold the corners so that they overlap evenly, centered on the crease mark. Unfold.

4 Unfold the bill.

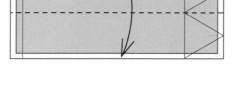

5 Valley-fold along the open ends of the triangles formed by the crease pattern. Unfold. Valley-fold a narrow margin at the opposite end of the bill. Unfold. (Use the measure of the first margin to make identical margins on the other bills.)

6 Valley-fold lengthwise.

7 Use the creases to inside-reverse-fold the indicated folded corner.

8 View toward the inside of the model.

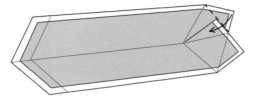

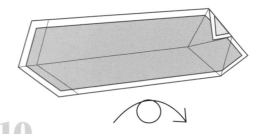

9 Press the inside-reversed corner against the left wall of the model. Valley-fold the top left flap over to hold it in place.

10 Your paper should look like this. Turn over.

X 3 or 4

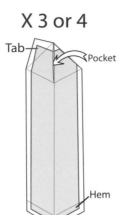

Tab —

Pocket

Hem

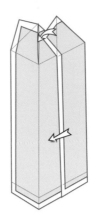

11 You will need 4 units for the classic monument, or use only 3 for a different look (or to add a second stage to Richie's Rocket, opposite). Notice the pocket and the tab on each unit.

12 Build the monument by sliding half of one unit over half of another. Tuck the tab of the outer unit into the pocket of the inner unit.

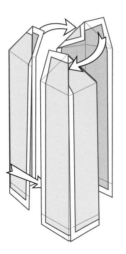

13 Continue adding units until you have enough for the desired style of monument.

14 Secure the monument by folding in the margins at the bottom.

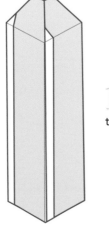

15 The George Washington Monument. Assemble multiple units and stack them to build higher and higher.

Richie's Rocket

Designed by Richard L. Alexander

For tips and gifts, we favor models we can fold quickly. Those especially useful have pockets or flaps to stash other singles. This simple rocket is quick to fold, and can be made with a triangular, square, or multi-faceted cross section, simply by adding elements. It is easily extended by stacking rockets, or topping with a George Washington Monument (page 14), and you can "fuel it up" with rolled up cash.

You will need at least three U.S. bills for one rocket.

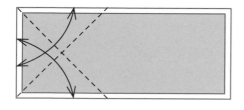

1 Valley-fold the short edge of the left end of the bill to the top long edge and to the bottom long edge, unfolding after each.

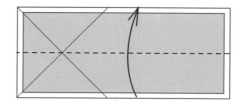

2 Valley-fold in half, long bottom edge to top.

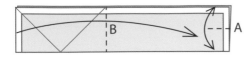

3 (A) Valley-fold a short crease at the middle of the right end. Unfold (B) Valley-fold the left end to the right, folding at the point where the ascending diagonal crease ends.

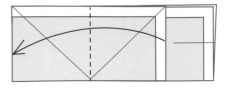

4 Valley-fold the right edge of the front flap to the left edge of the paper.

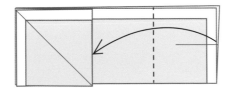

5 Valley-fold the right edge of the back flap to the folded edge of the front flap.

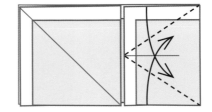

6 Valley-fold the corners of the right flap so that they overlap evenly, centered on the crease mark.

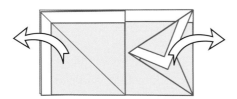

7 Unfold the bill completely.

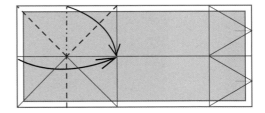

8 Use the crease pattern to inside-reverse-fold the top left side of the bill.

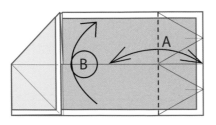

9 (A) Valley-fold and unfold the right-side vertical crease. (B) Turn over, bottom to top.

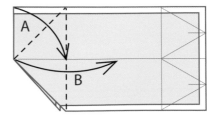

10 (A) Valley-fold the top left corner flap down. (B) Valley-fold the left-side vertical crease.

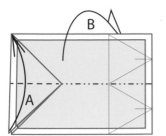

11 (A) Valley-fold the bottom left triangle flap up. (B) Mountain-fold in half, lengthwise.

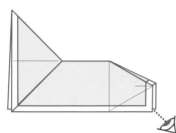

13 View toward the inside of the model.

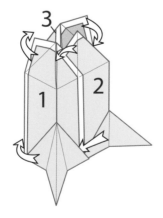

15 Turn the bill over.

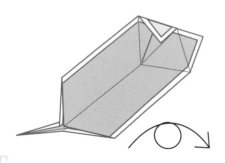

17 Assemble a rocket by overlapping the units and tucking the tabs into the pockets.

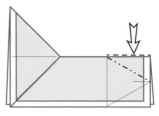

12 Use the creases to inside-reverse-fold the indicated corner.

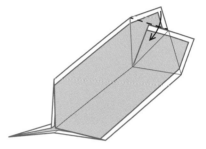

14 Press the inside-reversed corner against the left wall of the model. Valley-fold the top left flap over to hold it in place.

X3

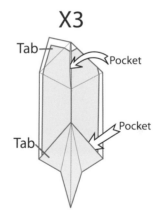

16 The completed unit. You will need at least three. Notice the location of the tabs and pockets.

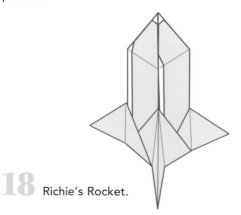

18 Richie's Rocket.

Two-Dollar Crown

Designed by Richard L. Alexander

Whether you use this as a blossom, pedestal, place card holder, or as an element to a dollar tower, this versatile abstract form is fun to fold and interesting to ponder.

You will need two U.S. bills.

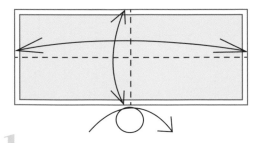

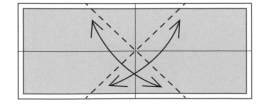

1 Begin with the reverse side up. Valley-fold in half, edge to edge, both ways, unfolding after each. Turn over, left to right.

2 Valley-fold 45 degrees diagonally, both ways, at the center of the bill, unfolding after each.

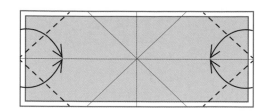

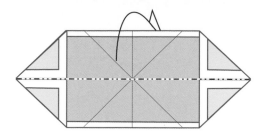

3 Valley-fold each of the four corners to meet at the horizontal center line.

4 Mountain-fold in half, lengthwise.

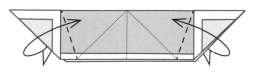

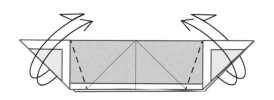

5 Valley-fold from the square corner of each triangle flap to the nearby bottom end of the 45 degree angle crease. Make these folds flexible by folding to the front and then to the back, several times.

6 Use the creases formed in step 5 to out-side-reverse-fold both ends of the model.

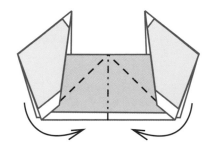

X 2

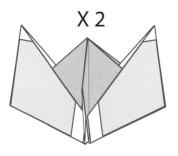

7 Use the creases at the middle of the model to form the crown shape.

8 You will need two folded elements to make one crown.

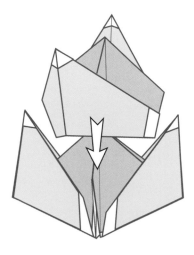

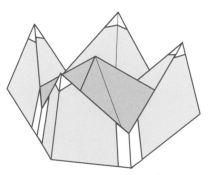

9 Orient the tines of one crown to be 90 degrees to the other. Nest one inside the other.

10 The Two-Dollar Crown.

Prosperity Bamboo

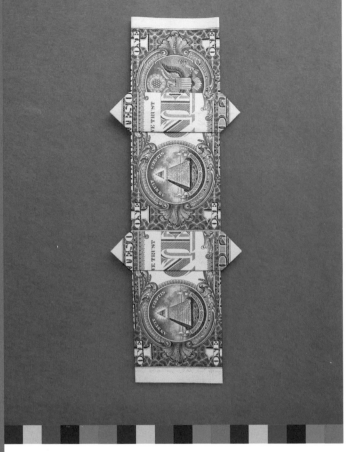

Designed by Michael G. LaFosse

Hawai'i has the perfect climate for bamboo, and this long, strong grass (and its remarkable fiber) is being used in everything from sturdy flooring to absorbent and comfortable clothing. Bamboo motif decorations put us in vacation mode. Use this cash bamboo to grace a card or package. The green color of the bills is perfect for displaying your wealth as a wall mural—a bamboo forest that can be grown or harvested as your needs change.

You will need at least two bills for one stalk of bamboo. Additional bills can be folded for leaves. See "Bamboo - Orchid Leaves," page 24.

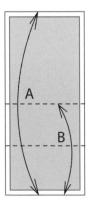

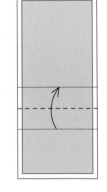

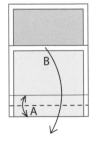

1 (A) Valley-fold the bill in half, short edge to short edge. Unfold. (B) Valley-fold the bottom edge to the center crease. Unfold.

2 Valley-fold the bottom edge up and lay the lower crease upon the upper crease, folding the distance between the two creases in half.

3 (A) Valley-fold the bottom folded edge up to the crease. Unfold. (B) Unfold the bill completely.

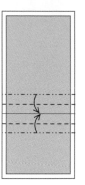

4 Use the crease pattern to form two pleats that meet edge to edge.

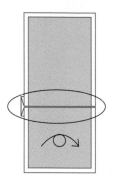

5 Your paper should look like this. Turn the paper over, left to right. Detail follows.

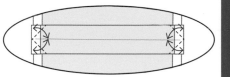

6 Valley-fold each of the four corners of the pleat to meet, edgewise, at the horizontal crease. Unfold.

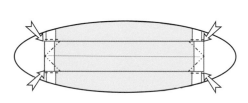

7 Inside-reverse-fold each corner to form the details for the joint.

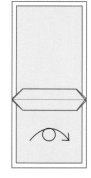

8 Your paper should look like this. Turn it over, left to right.

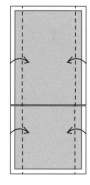

9 Valley-fold the left and right edges in. You will find the correct limit by the configuration of the outer corners of the joint.

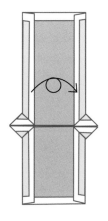

10 Your paper should look like this. Turn it over, left to right.

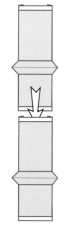

11 Insert the short, bottom end of one segment into the long, top end of another.

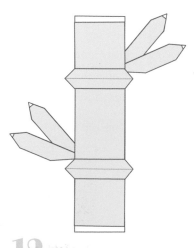

12 Prosperity Bamboo with added Bamboo Leaves, page 24.

Bamboo - Orchid Leaves

Designed by Michael G. LaFosse

Floral money folds usually focus on the blossom, but watch how your work will stand out if you add some money leaves. This simple design works well with our bamboo stalk, or with the Orchid blossom presented on page 26.

One bill forms two leaves.

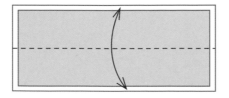

1 Valley-fold lengthwise. Unfold.

2 Valley-fold the long edges to meet at the middle.

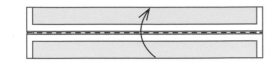

3 Valley-fold lengthwise.

4 Mark the middle of each end of the folded bill with a short valley crease.

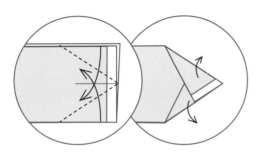

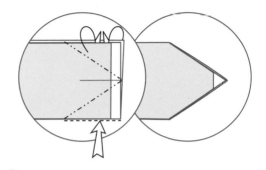

5 Valley-fold the corners so that they overlap evenly, centered on the crease mark. Unfold.

6 Use the creases to inside-reverse-fold the indicated folded corner. Mountain-fold the two corner flaps inside to lock the corner. Repeat at the other end of the paper.

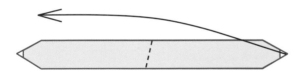

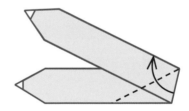

7 Valley-fold one end across to the other side, at an angle, displaying two leaves.

8 Valley-fold the bottom corner up.

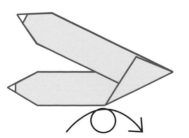

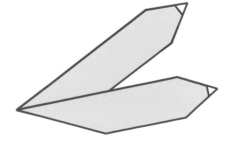

9 Turn over.

10 The Bamboo - Orchid Leaves.

Orchid

Designed by Michael G. LaFosse

Giving cash as part of any graduation gift is wildly popular in Hawaiʻi, and when the cash can be folded into floral subjects and presented as *leis* (big necklaces), the gesture is even more greatly appreciated. This orchid was designed after we visited a *lei*-making weekend workshop in Honolulu. Add this design to your collection of dollar bill flowers, and spread the wealth.

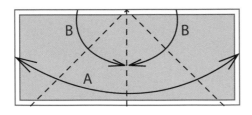

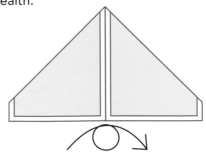

1 Begin with the obverse side up. (A) Valley-fold in half, short edge to short edge. Unfold. (B) Valley-fold each half of the top long edge to meet at the center crease.

2 Turn over, left to right.

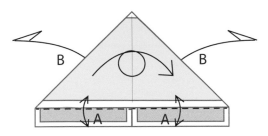

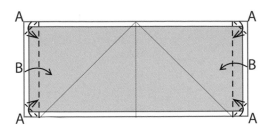

3 (A) Valley-fold the bottom flaps up. Unfold. (B) Unfold, then turn the bill over, left to right.

4 (A) Valley-fold each of the four corners, edge-wise, to the nearest crease. (B) Valley-fold the side flaps over.

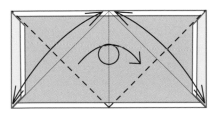

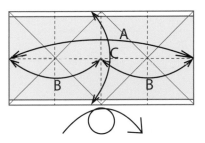

5 Valley-fold the missing diagonal crease in each half. Unfold and turn over, left to right.

6 (A) Valley-fold in half, short edge to short edge. Unfold. (B) Valley-fold the short edges to meet in the middle. Unfold. (C) Valley-fold, long edge to long edge. Unfold. Turn over, left to right.

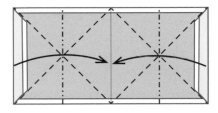

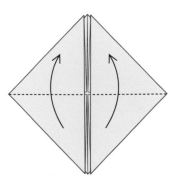

7 Use the mountain and valley creases to collapse each half of the model into layered triangles. Look ahead at the next diagram for the shape.

8 Valley-fold the bottom triangle flaps up.

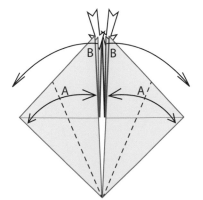

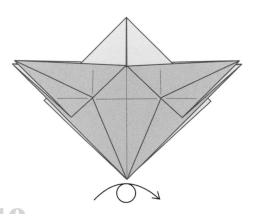

9 (A) Valley-fold the bottom edges to meet at the middle. Unfold. (B) Use the hinges from crease A to move each set of the top triangle flaps out, squash-folding the connecting layer of each set. Look at the next diagram for the shape.

10 Your paper should look like this. Turn it over, left to right.

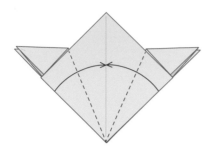

11 Valley-fold the bottom edges to meet at the middle.

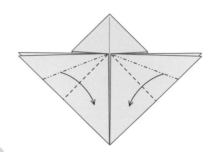

12 Squash-fold the top left and right triangle flaps.

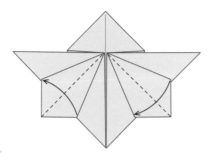

13 Valley-fold each kite-shape in half: Left up and right down.

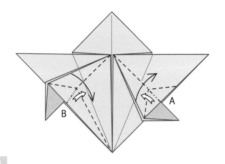

14 (A) Inside-reverse-fold the lower end of the free edge of the right-side kite while folding the flap back into place. (B) Inside-reverse-fold the full length of the free edge of the left-side kite while folding the flap back into place.

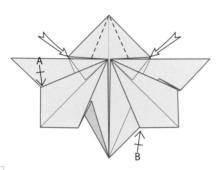

15 Repeat A on the left and B on the right. Inside-reverse-fold the left and right halves of the top flap.

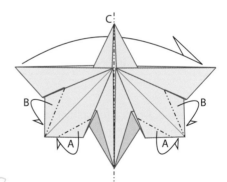

16 (A) Mountain-fold the bottom short edges of each kite. (B) Mountain-fold the top short edge of each kite. (C) Mountain-fold in half.

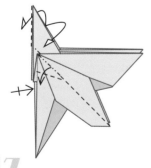

17 Mountain- and valley-fold the front middle point to form a crimp. Repeat behind. Outside-reverse-fold the right-side point up.

18 (Front view) Open the layers of the bottom point to shape the lip.

19 The Orchid.

Sitting Bunny

Designed by Michael G. LaFosse

A few years ago, we came across two orphaned, wild baby bunnies. Each was about the size of a walnut, and with eyedroppers, canned cat's milk, and a bag of bunny chow, we helped them grow big enough to be released. Michael brought "Nibbles" and "Walnut" to his origami events to explain how we enjoy carefully studying actual creatures before designing origami renditions. While with us, they attended several exclusive schools, famous libraries, and even a world-class muse-um—all without paying admission or tuition. Quite a prestigious *pet*-igree!

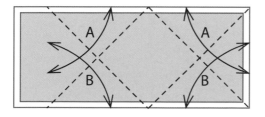

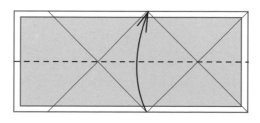

1 Begin obverse side up. (A) Valley-fold the short edge of the right side to the top edge, forming a right-triangle flap. Valley-fold the bottom left edge to align with the vertical edge of the triangle flap. Unfold. (B) Mirror the upward-oriented folds described in part A of this step, this time folding downward.

2 Valley-fold in half, long edge to long edge.

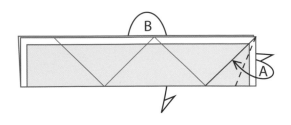

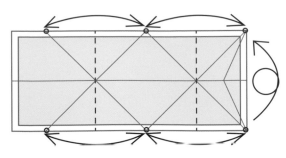

3 (A) Valley-fold the short right edge to the indicated crease. Unfold and fold to the back, exercising the crease. Unfold. (B) Move the back layer down, unfolding the bill, reverse side up.

4 Install two vertical valley-folds by folding each "X" in half. Unfold. Turn the paper over, bottom to top.

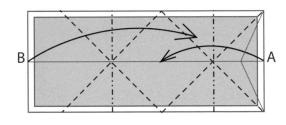

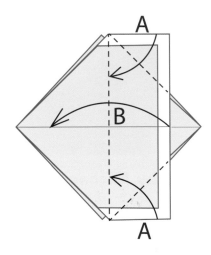

5 Use the mountain and valley creases to collapse the "Xs" into layered triangle shapes, A side first, then the B side.

6 Your paper should look like this. (A) Valley-fold the square corners edge-wise to the vertical center of the model. (B) Valley-fold the top flap to the left.

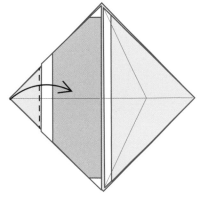

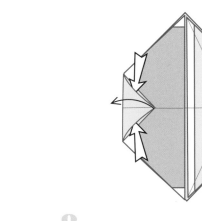

7 Valley-fold the left corner over the left edge of the flap.

8 Open the pockets of the triangle flap to puff open the paper for the tail.

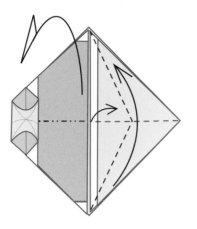

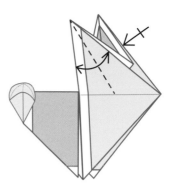

9 Mountain-fold the top half of the body layers down. Follow the creases to inside-reverse-fold the free edge of the right-side triangle layer while valley-folding the bottom corner of the triangle up.

10 Install valley creases by folding the back edges of the ears to the front edges, unfolding after each.

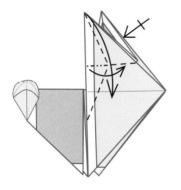

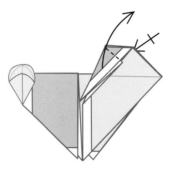

11 Use the valley creases to inside-reverse-fold the back edge of each ear while folding the top corner down.

12 Valley-fold the ears up.

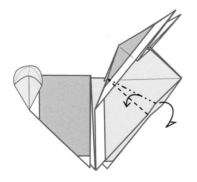

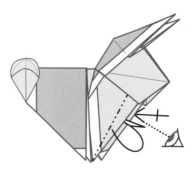

13 Mountain- and valley-fold a crimp on each side of the bunny's neck, bending the head downward.

14 Mountain-fold the leading edges of the front legs in. Inside view detail follows.

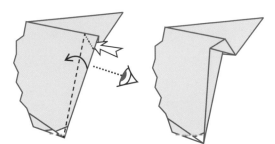

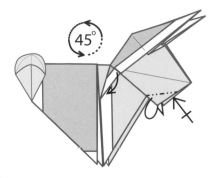

15 Notice that a small, accommodating squash fold is added at the top of the fold, inside the model.

16 Mountain-fold the bottom corners of the head in. Rotate the model 45 degrees counter-clockwise.

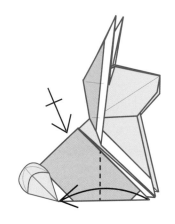

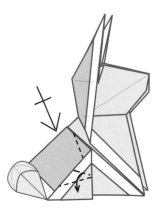

17 Form a foot flap by valley-folding the bottom front corner to the back end of the model, near the beginning of the tail. Repeat behind.

18 Valley- and mountain-fold a crimp at the top edge of the foot flap, swiveling and squashing the layer behind as it follows along. Repeat behind.

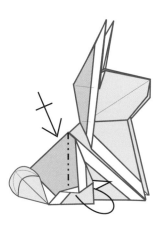

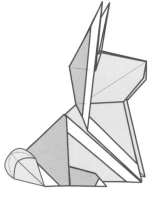

19 Mountain-fold the foot flap to rotate the foot point forward. Repeat behind.

20 "Walnut," our seated bunny.

Standing Bunny

Designed by Michael G. LaFosse

Animals often watch for predators by taking turns grazing while another stands guard as a lookout to carefully watch and listen. (The pairs of Canada Geese that visit us in the springtime along the Merrimack River do the same.)

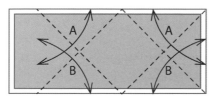

1 Begin obverse side up. (A) Valley-fold the short edge of the right side to the top edge, forming a right-triangle flap. Valley-fold the bottom left edge to align with the vertical edge of the triangle flap. Unfold. (B) Mirror the upward-oriented folds described in part A of this step, this time folding downward.

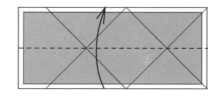

2 Valley-fold in half, bottom edge to top.

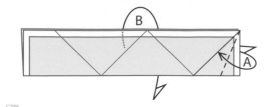

3 A) Valley-fold the short right edge to the indicated crease. Unfold and fold to the back, exercising the crease. Unfold. (B) Move the back layer down, unfolding the bill, reverse side up.

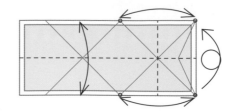

4 Valley-fold the right side "X" set of creases in half vertically. Unfold. Valley-fold the bottom edge to the top and unfold, reversing the crease. Turn the paper over, bottom to top.

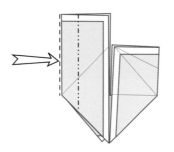

5 Use the crease pattern to outside-reverse-fold the right and left portions of the bill up. Look ahead at the next diagram for the shape.

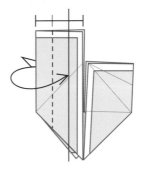

6 Valley-fold one-third of the left edge of the long, left portion over. Unfold and mountain-fold to the back, exercising the crease. Unfold.

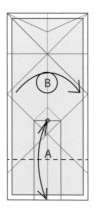

7 Push in on the creased area to sink the outer third portion of the left side of the model.

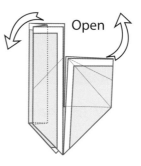

8 Open the paper completely and position the bill as shown in the next diagram.

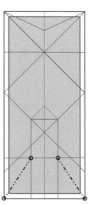

9 (A) Valley-fold the bottom edge up to the level of the crease, indicated by the red circle. Unfold. (B) Turn the paper over, left to right.

10 Install two mountain folds, each spanning the distance between the points indicated by the red circles.

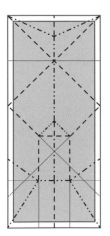

11 Use the crease pattern to mountain- and valley-fold the bill, collapsing to the form displayed in the next diagram.

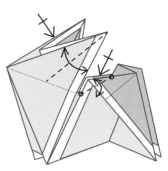

12 Install valley creases in the ears by folding the back edges to the front, unfolding after each. Valley-fold the corner at the top of the thighs, between the indicated points, unfolding after each.

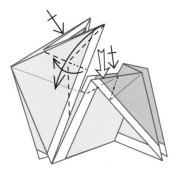

13 Inside-reverse-fold the back edges of the ears while folding the top corners down. Inside-reverse-fold the top corners of the hips.

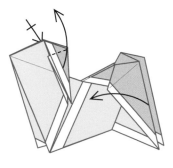

14 Valley-fold the ears up. Open the back end.

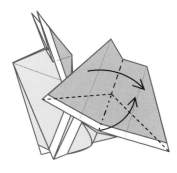

15 Inside-reverse-fold the bottom edge up and close the back end.

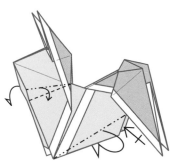

16 Mountain- and valley-fold a crimp on each side of the bunny's neck, bending the head downward. Mountain-fold the bottom edge of the body inside the model. Repeat behind.

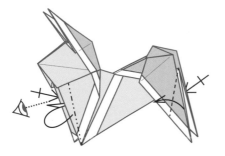

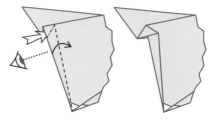

17 Form a foot flap by valley-folding the hind leg forward. Repeat behind. Mountain-fold the leading edges of the front legs in. Inside view detail follows.

18 Notice that a small, accommodating squash fold is added at the top of the fold, inside the model.

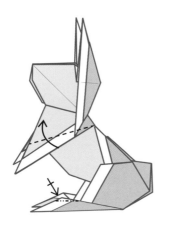

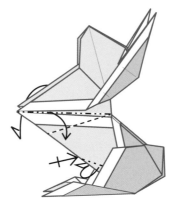

19 Mountain-fold the bottom corners of the head in. Untuck the trapped layers at the back of the head. Valley-fold the top edges of the foot flaps to the bottom edges. Rotate the model 90 degrees clockwise.

20 Form the arms with mountain and valley folds, crimping the paper down. Mountain-fold the edges of the lower abdomen in.

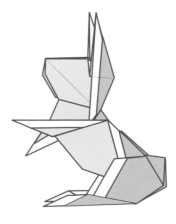

21 Valley-fold the front arm up. Mountain-fold the top corners of the feet down.

22 "Nibbles," our standing bunny.

George Washington Knot

Designed by Richard L. Alexander

This simple twist puts Georgie's mug in the middle, and becomes a decorative element that can be linked, tucked, curled as a ring, closed as a pouch, or simply used to decorate a stack of cash left as a tip.

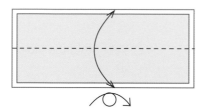

1 Begin with the reverse side up. Valley-fold in half, long bottom edge to top. Unfold and turn over, left to right.

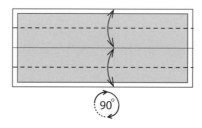

2 Valley-fold the long edges to meet at the center crease. Unfold and rotate the paper 90 degrees.

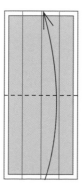

3 Valley-fold in half, short edge to short edge.

4 Install short valley creases by folding the bottom folded edge to align with each of the vertical creases, sequentially, unfolding after each. Turn over, left to right.

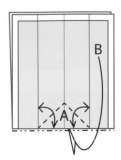
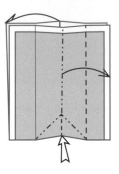

5 (A) Exercise the installed creases from the previous step by valley-folding and unfolding. (B) Mountain-fold the front flap to the back.

6 Push in at the center of the bottom folded edge and then use the installed creases to collapse the bill into the form shown in the next diagram.

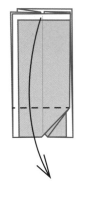
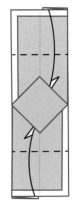
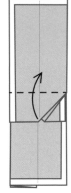

7 Valley-fold the front flap down.

8 Turn the paper over, left to right.

9 Valley-fold the indicated flap up.

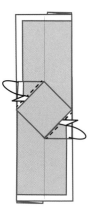
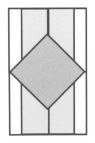

10 Valley-fold the triangle flaps under the center square.

11 Valley-fold the short edges of the top and bottom flaps under the center square.

12 The George Washington Knot. Make a "money clip" by mountain-folding the flaps in step 11 behind a stack of bills.

Reef Pony

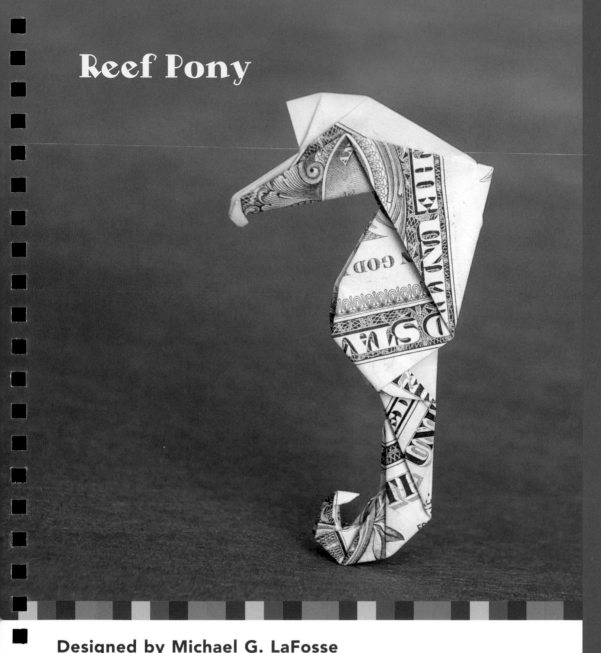

Designed by Michael G. LaFosse

Al Miyatake loaned us the art from the OrigamiUSA Christmas Tree (theme: The Sea Around Us, a.k.a the "Fishmas Tree") that had been exhibited at the Japan Airlines terminal in Kona, HI. We had made handmade paper for several of the fifty artists who created sea creatures for the exhibit, but one creature was clearly missing: an origami sea horse. (We later found out that there was once a seahorse on the tree in Kona, but that it "disappeared.") Michael set out to correct that omission, and came up with this delightful dollar bill origami sea horse that we named the Reef Pony. This led him to create a whole series of wonderful and elegant sea horse designs folded from squares.

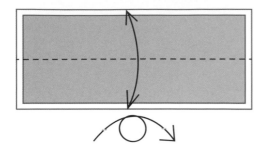

1 Valley-fold a bill in half, long edge to long edge. Unfold and turn it over, left to right.

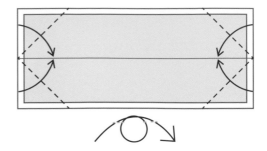

2 Valley-fold each of the four corners, edgewise to the center crease. Turn over, left to right.

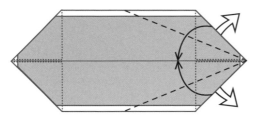

3 Valley-fold the folded edges of the right end to meet at the middle. Allow the triangle flaps from the back to come to the front.

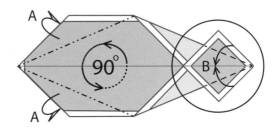

4 (A) Mountain-fold the folded edges of the left end to the center crease. (B) Valley-fold the outside edges of the right end to the center. Rotate the model 90 degrees counterclockwise. Detail view follows.

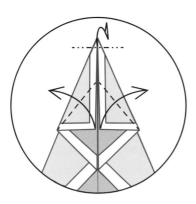

5 Mountain-fold the tip of the model behind. Valley-fold the square corners of the top triangle flaps out.

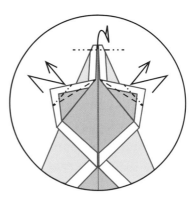

6 Mountain-fold another small portion of the tip of the model behind. Mountain- and valley-fold the square corners of the top triangle flaps to complete the head fins.

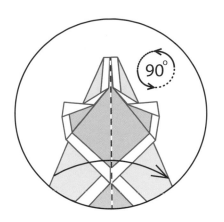

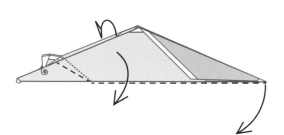

7 Valley-fold the model in half and rotate it 90 degrees counterclockwise.

8 Outside-reverse-fold the body.

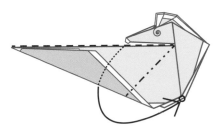

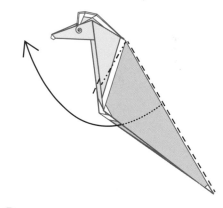

9 Inside-reverse-fold the body, aligning the folded spine of the larger portion with the bottom edge of the head.

10 Inside-reverse-fold the body, aligning the spine of the larger portion with the indicated corner.

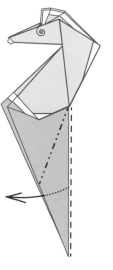

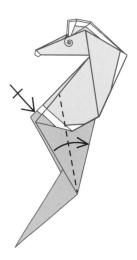

11 Inside-reverse-fold the tail.

12 Valley-fold the front edge of the model to the back edge of the tail. Repeat behind.

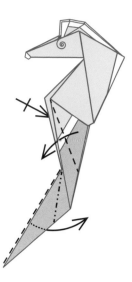

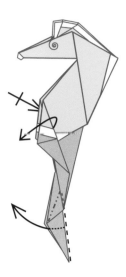

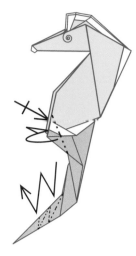

13 Valley-fold the free corner of the top flap beyond the front edge of the abdomen. Inside-reverse-fold the tail back.

14 Untuck the hidden flap of the top layer of the abdomen. Repeat behind. Inside-reverse-fold the tail forward.

15 Mountain-fold the bottom edges of the abdomen in. Mountain- and valley-fold the remaining length of the tail to form two more crimps to continue the curl.

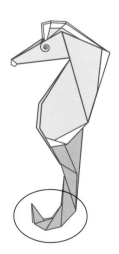

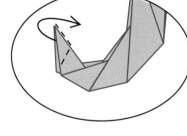

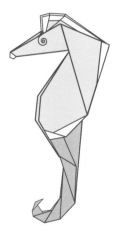

16 Detail follows.

17 Outside-reverse-fold the tip of the tail.

18 The Reef Pony.

American Shad

![American Shad origami made from a dollar bill]

Designed by Michael G. LaFosse

The old-timers know just when to set out shad jigs: "When the river runs clear and the new elm leaves are the size of a mouse's ear, good fishin's to be had with the running of the shad." The Merrimack drains about 5,000 square miles of lake and valley south of Mount Washington. It was home to several *anadromous* fish (ocean-going fish that return to rivers during some part of their life cycle). The Anadromous Fish Restoration Program is trying to bring back the rare Atlantic Salmon, Striped Bass, Shortnose Sturgeon, River Herring, and—our subject—the mighty, fighty American Shad, *Alosa sapidissima*. Sadly for these efforts, acidification and rising temperatures are taking a toll on these fish, and recently the numbers of returning adults have been decreasing.

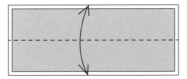

1 Begin obverse side up. Valley-fold in half, bottom long edge to top. Unfold.

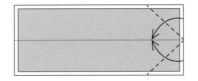

2 Valley-fold the two right-side corners, edge-wise, to meet at the crease.

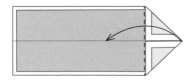

3 Valley-fold the triangle flap to the left.

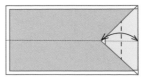

4 Valley-fold the square corner of the triangle to the center of its opposite edge (hypotenuse). Unfold.

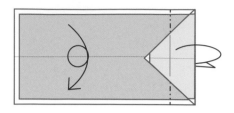

5 Mountain-fold the right edge behind, folding along the alignment of the vertical crease. Turn the bill over, top to bottom.

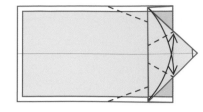

6 Inside-reverse-fold the indicated corners. Look ahead to the next diagram for the resulting shape.

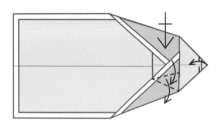

7 Valley-fold the triangle flap over and over to form a pectoral fin. Repeat on the other flap. Look at the next diagram for the shape. Valley-fold the tip of the triangle's square corner.

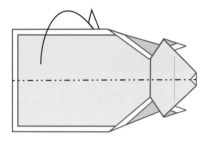

8 Mountain-fold in half lengthwise.

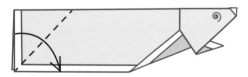

9 Valley-fold the short back edge to align with the bottom edge.

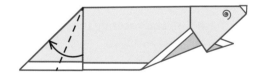

10 Valley-fold the short folded edge of the triangle flap to align with the long edge.

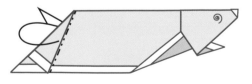

11 Mountain-fold the pleated triangle to the back.

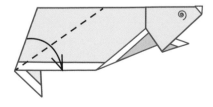

12 Valley-fold the back edge to align with the bottom edge.

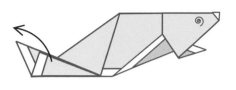

13 Unfold.

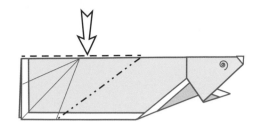

14 Inside-reverse-fold.

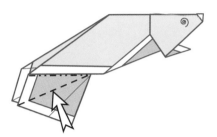

15 Inside-reverse-fold the front layer upward. Look ahead for the shape.

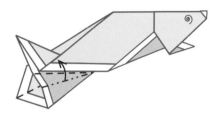

16 Squash-fold the lower half of the tail.

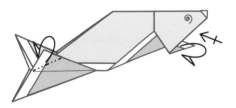

17 Mountain-fold the pectoral fins to point backward. Mountain-fold the square corner of the tail behind.

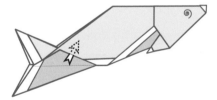

18 Tuck the resulting triangle flap under the body layer.

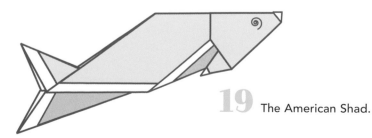

19 The American Shad.

Great Seal

Designed by Michael G. LaFosse

The U.S. one dollar bill bears the Great Seal of the United States on its back, and so it is fitting that Michael's origami Great Seal is designed to do the same. One of the most fascinating and mysterious—but threatened—marine mammals of the Hawai`ian Islands is the Monk Seal. Recently, scientists have begun fitting some seals with "critter cams" and they are just now beginning to learn what they eat, and how deep they must dive to feed.

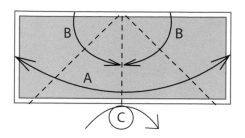

1 Begin with the reverse side up. (A) Valley-fold in half, short edge to short edge. Unfold. (B) Valley-fold each half of the top long edge down to align with the vertical crease. (C) Turn over, left to right.

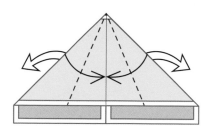

2 Valley-fold the left and right folded edges to the center crease, allowing the backside flaps to come to the front.

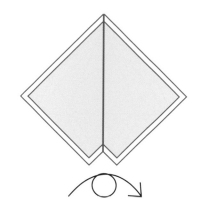

3 Turn over, left to right.

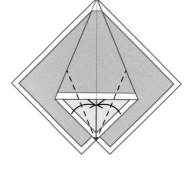

4 Valley-fold the bottom edges of the kite-shape to meet in the middle.

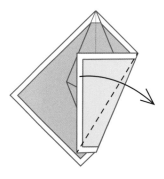

5 Valley-fold the right flap over the bottom-right folded edge.

6 Valley-fold the top flap diagonally.

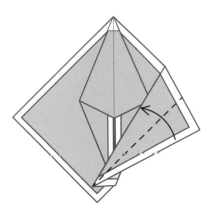

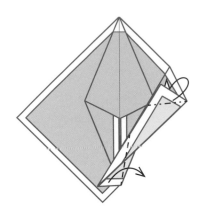

7 Valley-fold the long cut edge of the triangle flap to the long folded edge.

8 Mountain-fold the square corner of the top flap behind. Valley-fold the bottom corner to the right.

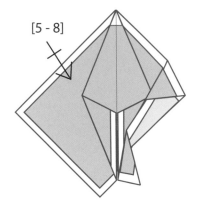

[5 - 8]

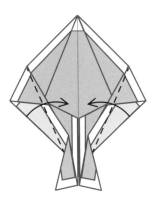

9 Repeat steps 5 through 8 on the left.

10 Valley-fold the left and right corners inward.

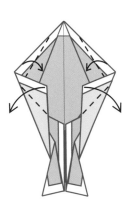

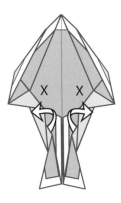

11 Valley-fold the obtuse corner of one of the top triangle flaps outward, while valley-folding the top edge in. Look ahead at the next diagram for the shape. Repeat on the other side.

12 Move the inside layers, marked with an X, out to cover the front flaps.

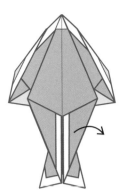

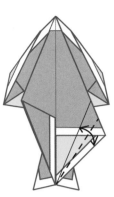

13 Open the bottom right flap only.

14 Valley-fold the long outside edge of the flap to the crease. Unfold.

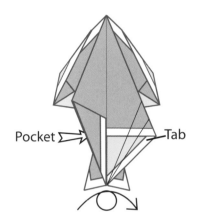

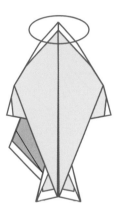

Pocket ⊐⇒ ⇐ Tab

15 Notice the "pocket," on the left, and the "tab," which is the outermost triangle segment on the right-side flap. You'll use these to close the belly of the seal at step 22. Turn over, left to right.

16 Head detail to follow.

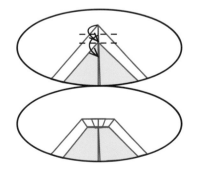

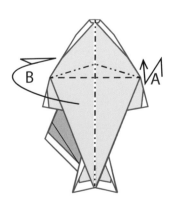

B ◄ A

17 Form the nose by valley-folding the tip of the head paper over twice.

18 (A) Valley-fold horizontally across the widest corners. (B) Mountain-fold in half, length-wise, while mountain-folding the top corner forward. Look ahead at the next diagram for the shape.

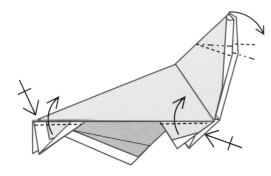

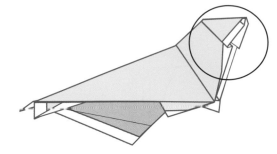

19 Valley-fold each of the four flippers upward. Valley- and mountain-fold at the neck-line to crimp the head downward.

20 Head detail to follow.

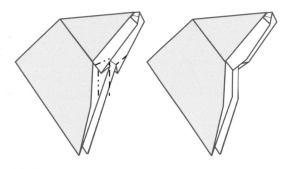

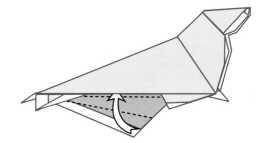

21 Mountain-fold the edges at the back-end of the jawline and the top edges of the chest.

22 Tuck the tab into the pocket, closing the belly.

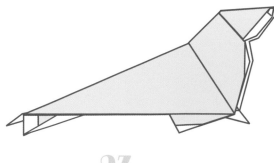

23 The Great Seal.

Teddy Bear

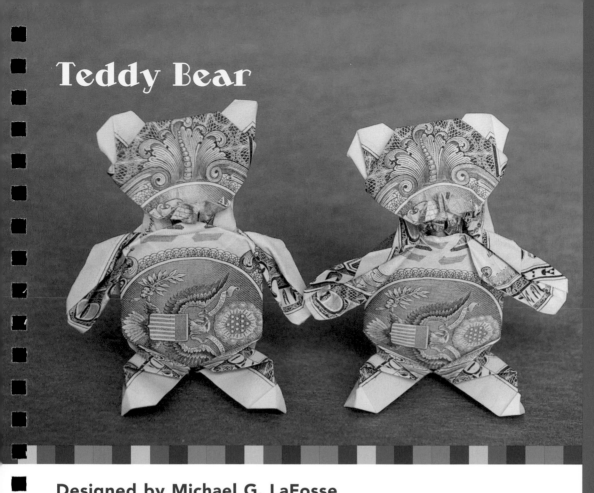

Designed by Michael G. LaFosse

We entertain numerous commercial requests for advertising origami, and one client needed an iconic image for their child-related services. While this design almost met their needs, one criteria was that it be simple to fold. Sadly this bear takes care, so Michael filed the design away for you to enjoy now. Cuddle up!

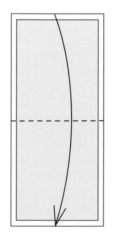

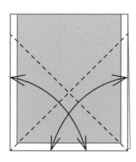

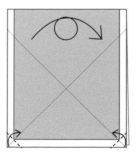

1 Begin reverse side up. Valley-fold in half, short edge to short edge.

2 Have the folded edge be the top edge. Valley-fold the bottom end of the top layer diagonally both ways, unfolding after each.

3 Valley-fold a small amount of the two bottom corners of the top layer over to form small triangles. Turn over, left to right.

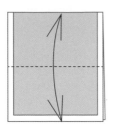

4 Valley-fold the bottom edge of the top layer up to the folded edge. Unfold.

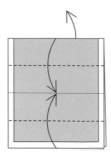

5 Valley-fold the bottom edge of the top layer to the center crease. Valley-fold the folded edge to the center crease, allowing the back layer to come to the front.

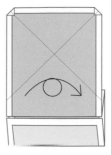

6 Turn over, left to right.

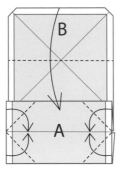

7 (A) Valley-fold the four indicated edges to the crease. (B) Valley-fold the top edge down, making the new fold pass horizontally through the intersection of the crossing diagonal creases.

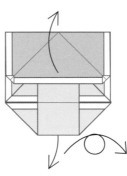

8 Open the paper completely, turn it over and position the bill as shown in the next diagram.

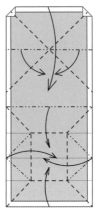

9 Use the mountain and valley creases to collapse the bill into the form illustrated in step 10.

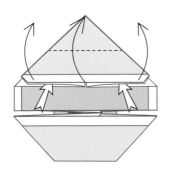

10 Open the layers where the white arrows indicate and fold the middle of the bottom edge up to the top corner. Flatten the shape to resemble the next figure.

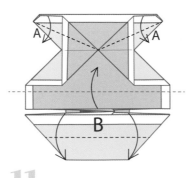

11 (A) Valley-fold the indicated layers to open the ears. (B) Open and flatten a box-shape by valley-folding the top layers of the trapezoid to the bottom edge and the upper horizontal folded edge upward.

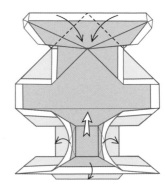

12 Step 11 in progress. Notice that the vertical walls will follow. Continue to move all four edges outward and flatten into a rectangular frame.

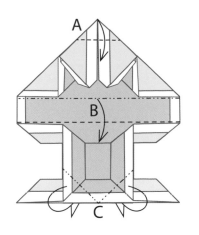

13 (A) Valley-fold the top corner down. (B) Mountain-fold at the horizontal base of the upper triangular area and valley-fold down, covering the top edge of the folded frame. (C) Mountain-fold the bottom left and right flaps behind, so that they will be vertical on the other side.

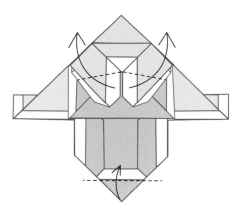

14 Valley-fold the ears up. Valley-fold the bottom corner up.

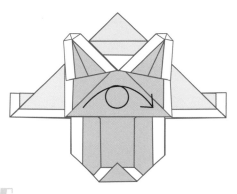

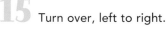

15 Turn over, left to right.

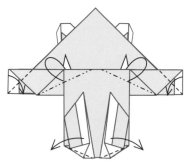

16 Mountain-fold the top edges of the central trapezoid behind. Valley-fold the left and right corners of the arms down. Valley-fold the legs out at the bottom.

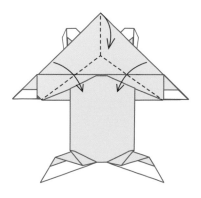

17 Simultaneously valley-fold the left and right edges of the top triangular area downward and to the front, folding the top-facing layer of the square corner in half and moving the head downward.

18 Open the space indicated by the white arrow and push the front end of the head down, flattening the face.

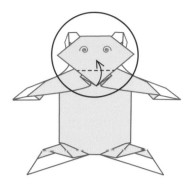

19 Valley-fold the bottom corner of the face up until the under layers stretch into the shape of two tall triangles, meeting at their longest edges.

20 Open each side of the muzzle where the white arrows indicate. Pull the muzzle forward and downward, stretching the nose open and forming a 3-D muzzle.

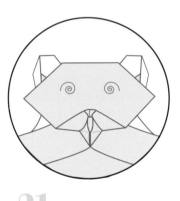

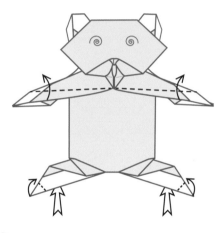

21 The completed face.

22 Valley-fold the front edges of the arms up to open. Open the legs from underneath and valley-fold the corners of the feet to the top side.

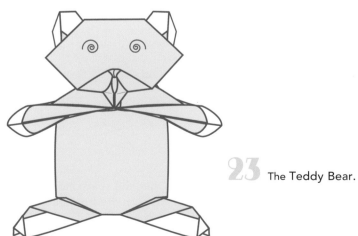

23 The Teddy Bear.

Standing Eagle

Designed by Michael G. LaFosse

Michael struck an Art Deco pose with this iconic American motif, which works well with the Art Deco elements of the bill's engraving. A bold, modern aesthetic that has been influential since the 1930s, Art Deco is an enduring ornamental style that seems to embrace technology. Some Art Deco hood ornaments from antique cars now are worth more than the cars when they were new.

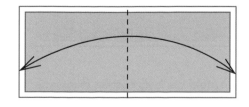

1 Begin obverse side up. Valley-fold in half, short edge to short edge. Unfold.

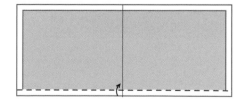

2 Valley-fold the bottom margin—defined by the print line—of the long edge up.

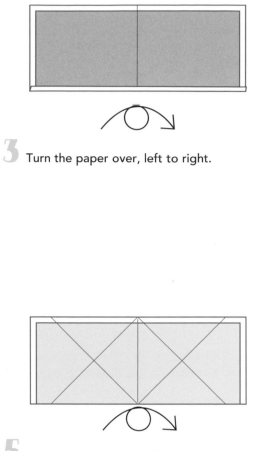

3 Turn the paper over, left to right.

4 One at a time, valley-fold each half of a long edge to align with the vertical crease. Unfold after each.

5 Turn the paper over, left to right.

6 Valley-fold each "X" pattern in half vertically. Use the crease ends, indicated by the red circles, as landmarks for folding.

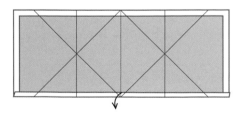

7 Unfold the bottom margin size.

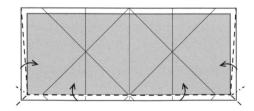

8 Valley-fold the long bottom margin up while folding the bottom corners in half. Valley-fold the short edges in, with the creases angling to intersect the top corners. Look at the next diagram for the shape.

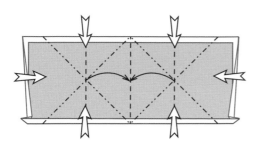

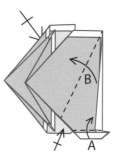

9 Use the crease pattern to collapse the bill into the form illustrated in the next diagram.

10 (A) Valley-fold the bottom trapezoid form up. Repeat behind. (B) Valley-fold the right edge over at an angle. Repeat behind. Look to the next diagram for the shape.

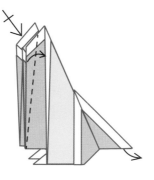

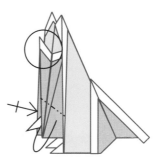

11 Valley-fold the leading edges of the wings over. Pull out the hidden corner at the end of the tail.

12 Mountain-fold the bottom corners of the body in. Detail of head to follow.

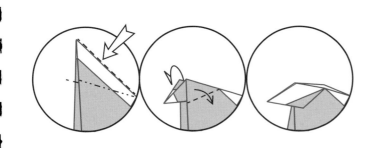

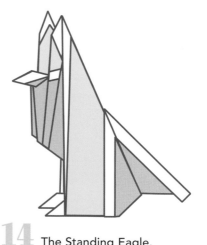

13 Inside-reverse-fold the head corner down. Outside-reverse-fold the head paper.

14 The Standing Eagle.

Three-Dollar Bird Base

Designed by Richard L. Alexander

We introduced this in one of our previous DVD kits, (*Mini Money Origami*, Tuttle Publishing), and it was so popular that we knew we should repeat the lesson to introduce an example of a more complex model. People do use a single bill with several adjustments to form a classic Bird Base, but the results are small and chunky. When you use three bills, the resulting models are much larger, and the additional edges and flaps can be put to good use when adding detail.

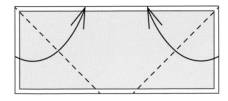

1 Wing Unit: Begin with the side of the bill that you wish to display facing up. Valley-fold the left and right short edges to the top long edge.

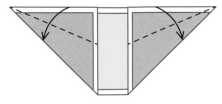

2 Valley-fold each of the two short edges to their adjacent folded edge.

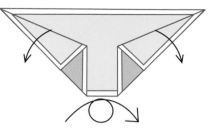

3 Move the triangle flaps out and turn the paper over, left to right.

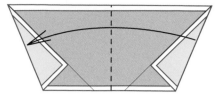

4 Valley-fold the paper in half by bringing the two folded edges together.

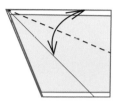

5 Valley-fold the top, long cut edge set to the crease. Unfold.

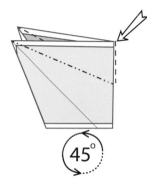

6 Inside-reverse-fold the triangle flap. Rotate the paper 45 degrees counterclockwise.

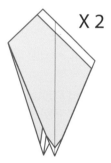

X 2

7 The completed Wing Unit. You will need two Wing Units for one bird base.

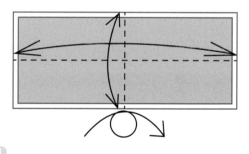

8 Center Unit: Begin with the preferred display side facing down. Valley-fold the paper in half edge to edge, both ways, unfolding after each. Turn over, left to right.

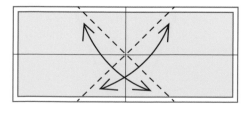

9 Valley-fold the paper in half diagonally at the center, 45 degrees, both ways, unfolding after each.

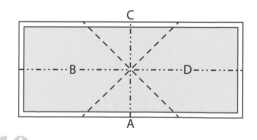

10 Use the mountain and valley creases to collapse the bill into the shape displayed in step 11. Each mountain crease has been labeled for reference.

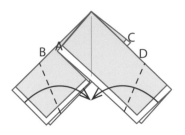

11 Organize the flaps to make your paper look like this. Valley-fold the bottom short edges to meet at the center.

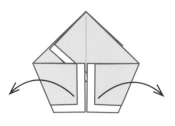

12 Your paper should look like this. Unfold.

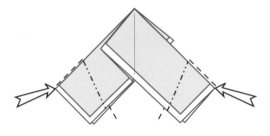

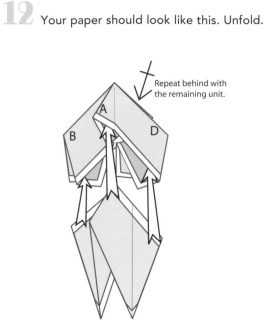

Repeat behind with the remaining unit.

13 Inside-reverse-fold the ends of the long flaps.

14 The completed Center Unit. Insert each of the wing units, as shown, to assemble the bird base.

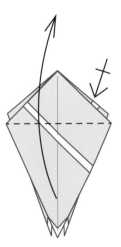

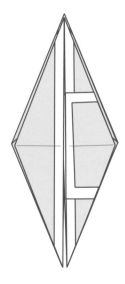

15 Valley-fold the front and the back flaps up.

16 The Three-Dollar Bird Base.

Drahcir the Dragon

Designed by Michael G. LaFosse

In one of our previous DVD money folding kits (*Mini Money Origami*, Tuttle Publishing) we introduced our Three-Dollar Bird Base, and proceeded to demonstrate a couple of subjects to fold from it. Here is yet another. Designed in the Year of the Dragon, Drahcir (Richard spelled backwards) is a delightful dollar dragon that provides wonderful opportunities to add details not possible when folding with a single bill.

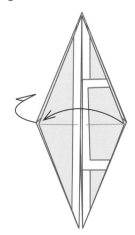

1 Begin with a Three-Dollar Bird Base, as described in the previous project. Move the top right layer to the left and the left back layer to the right.

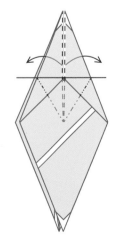

2 Inside-reverse-fold each of the two top points out, so that their highest point, at the top of the reverse, is level with the top center corner of the model.

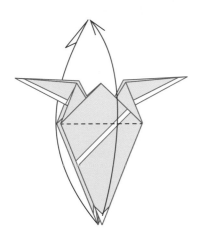

3 Valley-fold the front and back flaps up.

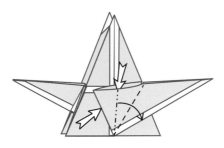

5 Squash-fold the flap symmetrically.

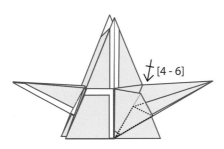

7 Repeat steps 4 through 6 on the other side.

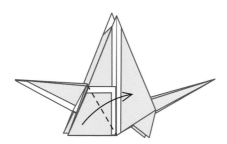

9 Valley-fold the bottom-left corner flap to the right, as far as it will go, flat.

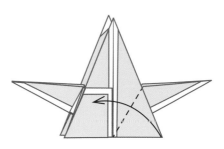

4 Valley-fold the bottom right corner flap to the left, as far as it will go, flat.

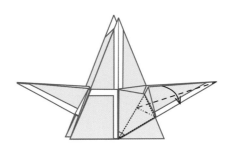

6 Inside-reverse-fold the top edge of the front layer of the right-side point down to the bottom edge.

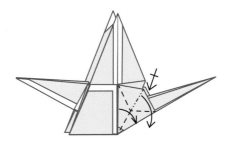

8 Form a rear leg by inside-reverse-folding the obtuse corner of the kite-shaped layer while folding the kite in half. Repeat behind.

10 Valley-fold the top right corner of the flap in half while valley-folding the adjacent edges over.

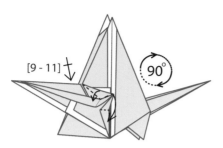

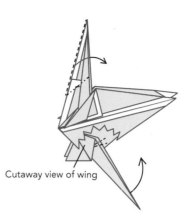

Cutaway view of wing

11 Valley-fold the outside layers of the folded corner to flatten the corner to point downward. Repeat steps 9 through 11 on the other side. Rotate the model 90 degrees.

12 Crimp the tail up so that Drahcir can stand. Inside-reverse-fold the top point back to form the neck.

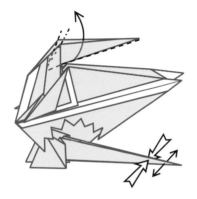

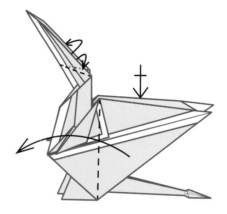

13 Inside-reverse-fold the neck up. Pinch the tail paper tightly near the end and open the layers from the underside, forming a spade-shaped tail-end.

14 Outside-reverse-fold the top of the neck to make paper for the head. Valley-fold the wings forward.

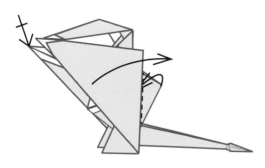

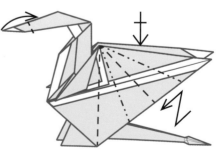

15 Valley-fold the back-protruding square corner point inside the model. Move the wing flaps back.

16 Outside-reverse-fold the tip of the head paper back. Pleat the wings into equal fourths, following the valley-mountain-valley-mountain pattern in the diagram.

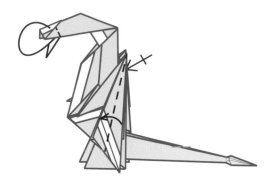

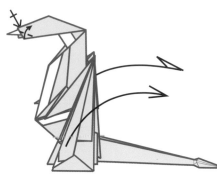

17 Mountain-fold the end of the head paper under and inside. Valley-fold the outer edge of the wing to align with the mountain fold edge. Repeat behind.

18 Open the wings.

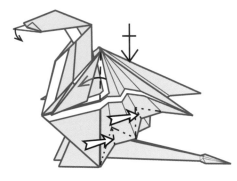

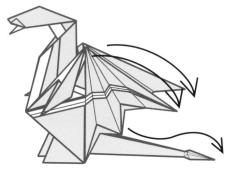

19 Pull down the protruding point at the end of the mouth. Valley-fold and hide the extraneous flap at the top of the wing. Inside-reverse-fold the bottom ends of the mountain fold pleats of the wings.

20 Add gently sweeping curves to the wings and the tail. Make any additional adjustments for poise and balance.

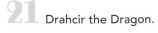

21 Drahcir the Dragon.